Every Body

Written by Tekla White

ELEMENTARY · SECONDARY · ADULT · LIBRARY

A Harcourt Company

www.steck-vaughn.com

We use our ears to hear.

We use our tongues to taste.

We use our eyes to see.

We use our hands to feel.

We use our noses to smell.

We use our legs to move.

We use our lips to smile!